S0-BRX-304

FOR I KNOW THE PLANS I HAVE FOR YOU,

SAYS THE LORD

ELLYN SANNA

God has marvelous plans for you, grad.

"*For* I know the plans I have for you,"
declares the LORD,
"plans to prosper you and not to harm you,
plans to give you hope and a future."

Jeremiah 29:11 NIV

© 2002 by Barbour Publishing, Inc.

ISBN 1-59310-614-9

All rights reserved. No part of this publication may be reproduced or transmitted in any form or by any means without written permission of the publisher.

The selection by Viola Ruelke Gommer is used with the author's permission.

Scripture quotations marked THE MESSAGE are taken from THE MESSAGE. Copyright © by Eugene H. Peterson 1993, 1994, 1995. Used by permission of NavPress Publishing Group.

Scripture quotations marked NIV are taken from the HOLY BIBLE, NEW INTERNATIONAL VERSION®. NIV®. Copyright © 1973, 1978, 1984 by International Bible Society. Used by permission of Zondervan. All rights reserved.

Scripture quotations marked NLT are taken from the Holy Bible, New Living Translation, copyright © 1996. Used by permission of Tyndale House Publishers, Inc. Wheaton, Illinois 60189, U.S.A. All rights reserved.

Scripture quotations marked KJV are taken from the King James Version of the Bible.

Cover image © PhotoDisc

Designed by Robyn Martins.

Published by Barbour Publishing, Inc., P.O. Box 719, Uhrichsville, Ohio 44683, www.barbourbooks.com

Our mission is to publish and distribute inspirational products offering exceptional value and biblical encouragement to the masses.

Member of the
Evangelical Christian
Publishers Association

Printed in China.
5 4 3 2 1

One

Never Settle for Less Than God's Best

God has marvelous plans for your life. Sometimes, though, we settle for less than God's everything. "I want to give you infinite blessings," He says to us. And we answer:

"But I don't deserve so much."
 "But I can't believe You mean it."
  "But I'm not talented enough."
   "But I'm too busy."

All our "buts" make a wall around our lives— a wall that keeps God's blessing out.

Don't limit what God wants to do in your life. Take what He has to offer.

"BUT" IS A FENCE OVER
WHICH FEW LEAP.

German Proverb

May Thy grace, O Lord,
make that possible to me which
seems impossible to me by nature.

Amy Carmichael

In the months and years to come, life will offer you many choices. Choose carefully. Some options will seem easier, while others will seem more challenging. Don't necessarily select the path of least resistance.

Instead, make the choices that will lead you to the deepest and fullest life. Don't be afraid to take risks. Choose to become all that God wants you to be.

Today you're ready for big challenges. You want to scale mountains, explore new lands, achieve feats that have never before been accomplished. Hold on to that courage and excitement.

For I promise you there will be mountains to climb, new lands to be explored, and new achievements to accomplish. But you will also face a different sort of challenge: ordinary days when there's not a mountain-top in sight. Face the monotony of humdrum daily life with the same courage and commitment you bring to life's mountain peaks. God has extraordinary plans for your ordinary life.

———

DO NOT WAIT FOR EXTRAORDINARY
SITUATIONS TO DO GOOD;
TRY TO USE ORDINARY SITUATIONS.

Jean Paul Richter

Don't let procrastination stand in the way of your achievement. Fear, laziness, and lack of focus tempt us all to avoid life's more difficult challenges. "Later," we promise ourselves, "when I have more education. . . when I make more money. . .when I have more time. . . when I'm older. . .when circumstances are better. . ."

Don't postpone life. If you do, you may miss out on God's best for you.

The wise does at once what the fool does at last.

Baltasar Gracián

What people say you cannot do,
you try and find that you can.

Henry David Thoreau

———

BE NOT AFRAID OF
GROWING SLOWLY;
BE AFRAID ONLY
OF STANDING STILL.

Chinese Proverb

———

A wise man will make more opportunities
than he finds.

Francis Bacon

HERE I AM, LORD—
BODY, HEART, AND SOUL.
GRANT THAT WITH YOUR LOVE,
I MAY BE BIG ENOUGH
TO REACH THE WORLD,
AND SMALL ENOUGH
TO BE AT ONE WITH YOU.

Mother Teresa

Two

Rely on God's Guidance

God guides us. . . .
He leads us step by step, from event to event.
Only afterward,
as we look back over the way we have come. . .
do we experience the feeling of having been led
without knowing it,
the feeling that God has mysteriously guided us.
Paul Tournier

*You will hear a voice say,
"This is the way;
turn around and walk here."*

Isaiah 30:21 NLT

The steps of the godly are directed by the LORD.
He delights in every detail of their lives.
Though they stumble, they will not fall,
for the LORD holds them by the hand.

Psalm 37:23–24 NLT

Sometimes we wish God would spell out His will for our lives in big block letters; we wish He would write it across the sky or broadcast it from some heavenly loudspeaker. We imagine that His plan looks like a neat, ten-point outline—or maybe a checklist we could post on our bulletin boards.

But really, God's plan for our lives is simply this: that we walk hand in hand with Him, each day, each moment. We find the fulfillment of His plan not in external events but in a living, growing relationship with the God who loves us.

Trust in the LORD with all your heart
and lean not on your own understanding;
in all your ways acknowledge him,
and he will make your paths straight.

Proverbs 3:5–6 NIV

O my Lord. . .so long as we love and obey You, we can be certain that You will direct us on the right path. And as we tread that path, we will know that it is Your power and love that have put us there.

. . .The path on which You have put me is a royal road, broad and smooth. It is safe for anyone who chooses to take it. And Your Son holds the hand of all who walk on it. If we become tired or discouraged, we need only look up to see Your smiling face in the distance, inviting us to share Your joy.

Teresa of Ávila

Sometimes we assume that God's plans for our lives are full of sacrifice and self-denial. And yes, God does ask us to deny those selfish, egotistical aspects of ourselves, the parts of us that insist on their own way, that whisper, "Me first!" But when we allow those demanding, sinful natures to die in Christ, we also find ourselves free for the first time. . . .

Free to enjoy all the delight and wonder God's world has to offer. . .

Free to be our truest selves. . .

Free to pursue our hearts' deepest desires. God's plans for us are better than any we could ever imagine.

I will lead the blind by ways they have not known,
along unfamiliar paths I will guide them;
I will turn the darkness into light before them
and make the rough places smooth.

Isaiah 42:16 NIV

YOU ARE HOLDING
MY RIGHT HAND.
YOU WILL KEEP ON GUIDING ME
WITH YOUR COUNSEL,
LEADING ME TO
A GLORIOUS DESTINY.

Psalm 73:23–24 NLT

THREE

ASK GOD FOR THE WISDOM TO DISCERN HIS PLAN FOR YOUR LIFE

Seek the LORD your God,
You will find him
if you look for him with all your heart
and with all your soul.

Deuteronomy 4:29 NIV

As you head into the life that lies ahead, you'll hear a whole chorus of conflicting voices offering you guidance.

"Do this," they'll shout; "you'll make more money."

"Do that," they'll whisper; "it's the only practical thing."

"You have to do this," others will croon; "everyone else is."

"This is your only choice," still others will insist; "otherwise people won't like you."

In all the uproar, God's voice will be so small and quiet you may miss it altogether. It will take time. . . and solitude. . .and silence to hear the gentle leading of His Spirit.

If we focus on worldly achievement or tangible rewards, we may miss the fullness of God's plans for our lives. God may choose to bless us with worldly prestige and material riches—or He may honor us just as richly with a humble life of quiet integrity. No matter the outward appearance of His plans, His Spirit will help us choose with wisdom the right paths for our lives. Whatever external route we follow, the secret is to keep our eyes fixed on Him. Then His deepest, loveliest plans will continue to unfold in the secrecy of our hearts.

THOUGH WE TRAVEL THE WORLD
OVER TO FIND THE BEAUTIFUL,
WE MUST CARRY IT WITH US
OR WE FIND IT NOT.

Ralph Waldo Emerson

Steer the ship of my life, good Lord, to Your quiet harbour. . . . Show me the course I should take. Renew in me the gift of discernment, so that I can always see the right direction I should go. And give me the strength and the courage to choose the right course, even when the sea is rough. . . .

Basil of Caesarea

———

If you take too long in deciding

what to do with your life,

you'll find you've done it.

George Bernard Shaw

Most merciful God, order my [life] so that I may know what You want me to do, and then help me to do it. Let me not be elated by success or depressed by failure. I want only to take pleasure in what pleases You. . . . Let my thoughts frequently turn to You, that I may be obedient to You without complaint, patient without grumbling, cheerful without self-indulgence, contrite without dejection, and serious without solemnity. Let me hold You in awe without feeling terrified of You, and let me be an example to others without any trace of pride.

Thomas Aquinas

Four

Trust God to Work All Things Together for Your Good

Be content with who you are,

and don't put on airs.

God's strong hand is on you;

he'll promote you at the right time.

Live carefree before God;

he is most careful with you.

1 Peter 5:6–7 The Message

We stand upon the verge of the unknown. . . . Who can tell what we shall find? What new experiences, what changes shall come, what new needs arise? But here is the cheering, comforting, gladdening message from our heavenly Father: "The Lord thy God careth for it" (Deuteronomy 11:12 KJV).

. . .Trust only. The Father comes near to take our hand and lead us on our way.

Mrs. Charles E. Cowman

God will never, never, never let us down
if we have faith and put our trust in Him.
He will always look after us.

Mother Teresa

YOU WILL KEEP IN PERFECT PEACE
ALL WHO TRUST IN YOU,
WHOSE THOUGHTS
ARE FIXED ON YOU!

Isaiah 26:3 NLT

Have faith in God. He will bring opportunity out of every crisis. His creative power did not end back in Genesis. Instead, He continually creates the world anew, weaving even the most devastating events into a pattern of glory.

The God who gave birth to the stars is still alive. He will work His plans to fruition in your life.

GRADUATION IS BOTH AN ENDING. . .AND A NEW BEGINNING.

Out of each ending comes a resurrection of something new. You are beginning a new journey in life, with new dreams and new hopes.

It is hard to let some things end in our lives—and yet growth demands it. Life dies only if we refuse to let go of some aspect of it. It crumbles only when we reject the mystery of endings—and beginnings.

For when we accept the endings we find new beginnings, new growth, and new challenges for the days ahead. You are on a new journey. You are beginning again.

Viola Ruelke Gommer

YOU CAN RELY ON GOD
TO PROSPER YOU. . .
AND NEVER HARM YOU. . .
TO GIVE YOU HOPE. . .
AND A FUTURE.

———

He has great things in store for you. Never settle for less than His best. Rely on His guidance. Ask Him for the wisdom to discern His plan for your life. And always trust Him to work all things together for your good. He will never let you down.